Five Steps Toward a Better Marriage

DAVID A. THOMPSON

BETHANY HOUSE PUBLISHERS
MINNEAPOLIS, MINNESOTA 55438
A Division of Bethany Fellowship, Inc.

Unless otherwise noted, Scripture quotations are taken from the Revised Standard Version of the Bible, copyrighted 1946, 1952 © 1971, 1973.

Five Steps Toward a Better Marriage

David A. Thompson

ISBN 0-87123-164-6

Published by Bethany Fellowship, Inc.
6820 Auto Club Road, Minneapolis, Minnesota 55438

Printed in the United States of America

Dedication

I dedicate this book to Judy, my wife, lover, and best friend: who, on the bare promise of love, dares to walk with me through sunshine and shadow "till death do us part."

About the Author

David A. Thompson is a chaplain serving in the United States Navy. He has been a parish pastor, hospital chaplain, Bible school teacher, and assistant editor for a religious book publisher.

He received a B.S. from the University of Wisconsin (Superior) in 1968; attended Trinity Evangelical Divinity School and the Lutheran Brethren Seminary, graduating from the latter with a M.Div. degree in 1971; and received a M.S.E. degree in Counseling from the University of Wisconsin (Oshkosh) in 1976. He is an ordained minister of the Free Methodist Church of North America.

He is married and the father of three boys.

The author has written a companion counseling guide for couples contemplating marriage entitled, *A Premarital Guide for Couples and Their Counselors* (Bethany Fellowship, Inc., 1979).

Table of Contents

How To Use This Book

FOR COUPLES: This book is designed to help couples enrich their marriage relationship by stimulating discussion on ways they can grow together. It is to be used by couples either by themselves or with a counselor or clergyman in individual or group settings.

If used alone, without professional help, I recommend that husbands and wives work on each section individually (except for the budget in Section III and the contract comparison sheets in Section V). Once completed, each should compare sheets with his/her partner, discussing patterns of compatibility/incompatibility which affect their relationship.

I would recommend, if possible, that this book be used with the assistance of a counselor or clergyman. Each section should be filled out and given to the counselor or clergyman, preferably a day or two before each session. This gives him the opportunity to become familiar with you and your needs. If used in a group setting, couples upon completing each section should compare their sheets with their spouse and be prepared to share their general observations with the group.

FOR COUNSELORS: This counseling guide is designed to be used in several ways. It can be used by pastors to encourage marital enrichment among their people. Couples can work through each section with the assistance of a counselor, work through the whole book on their own and then invite a pastor/counselor into their discussion, or work through each section as homework in preparation for a counselor-led group process of relational enrichment.

Another way this book can be used is in ministering to couples in conflict. As couples seek your counsel or are identified by you as having potential problems, this guide will prove to be a good tool in directing your discussion toward making things better.

I recommend that you use the five-session format as a guideline, being flexible to expand or contract the discussion according to the needs of the couple.

Individual Counseling

The couple should work on each section on their own (except the budget in Section III and the "contract negotiation" and "final contracts" in Section V, which should be done together). Prior to each session, have each counselee tear out the appropriate section and mail it to you in time to be received a day or two before each session. This will allow you time to review their responses and provide direction for your session together. As the couple prepares to leave following each session, briefly outline their "homework" for the next session.

If the couple has not used *A Premarital Guide for Couples and Their Counselors* prior to getting married, I suggest that you give them the historical summary found in Appendix I ("What We See in Our Past") in addition to the first assignment from Section I.

Group Counseling

When this guide is used in a relational enrichment group, it can serve as a basis for a general discussion on the topic area or can be utilized in a more direct manner by using the questions found in the "Group Leaders Discussion Guide" in Appendix II.

It is suggested that the group leader let the group set the pace, rather than woodenly adhering to a strict schedule which forces the group to get through each section in one sitting. The author recommends that group members start with Appendix I, which is historical data and rather nonthreatening in nature. Such a procedure will help group members share and assist the group leader in developing an accepting, nonthreatening community. This will enable the group to openly share their concerns on more difficult topics as the sessions progress.

It is recommended that the group stay one section ahead of the present discussion so as to provide a format to accelerate into the next section ahead of schedule. Each leader is then given the flexibility to pace the course to fit his/her time constraints. It is recommended that group sessions be spaced apart by one week to allow for assimilation of material and dialogue between each couple. Another possibility is to use the material during an intense weekend retreat emphasizing relational enrichment.

If possible, it is recommended to have two group facilitators lead the sessions (preferably a husband and wife team). One facilitator would directly lead the session and the other would assume an assisting reflective role, adding to content of dialogue and monitoring group dynamics.

Space is allowed under each section in the "Group Leaders Discussion Guide" (Appendix II) for the group leader to write comments, either in preparation for each session or in response to the dynamics that are being displayed while the group is in session.

Group leaders must encourage completion of the "homework" prior to each session. Each couple should bring their homework to each session for their own reference (sheets are not to be exchanged with other group members) to assist in stimulating meaningful group discussion. Retention of forms is encouraged for couples' future reference. If a couple feels that they have problems which require more intense attention than provided in the group process, these forms will help whomever the couple is referred to in providing informed assistance.

Group leaders should strongly encourage attendance at, and participation in, each session by group members. A "closed group" is recommended, not allowing new people into the group after it begins. Such a posture can, along with verbal reenforcement, develop a climate of trust and confidence which will stimulate more active and open participation by members.

It is suggested that each couple participating in the group pay a minimal fee to cover costs of their book and any other incidentals necessary to establish the program (i.e., refreshments, etc).

The author provides this guide for the assistance of couples and their counselors. He will not be responsible for how this guide is used. He trusts that it will be used to help couples discuss their marriage frankly and be instrumental in making their marriage better.

SECTION I

What We See in Each Other

"You did not choose me, but I chose you and appointed you that you should go and bear fruit and that your fruit should abide" (John 15:16, RSV).

Whether we remember them or not, there were some good reasons why we married that very special person in our life. We saw a quality of goodness in some area of our spouse's personality which drew us into their world. Yet, somehow, with the passage of time and the effects of stress, we lost sight of that special feature which first brought us together.

Jesus helps us to see the value in that "special other" person again. He shows us He has a plan for each one of us; to be fruitful and to be a blessing to others. It is important that we remember this truth and work toward encouraging His work of fruitbearing in the life of our spouse.

As you work through this portion of this marriage inventory, I encourage you to set aside some of the negative thoughts that may occupy your thinking. Instead, seek to rediscover some of the basic reasons why you were drawn toward each other. This is not an attempt to gloss over shortcomings; rather, it is a commitment to balance your perspective. May you see anew God's plan for fruitfulness in your relationship.

What We See in Each Other

Wife

Describe briefly your relationship to date in the following ways:

Positive experiences:

Negative experiences:

What premarital expectations have been fulfilled?

What premarital expectations have not been fulfilled?

In what ways have you changed since you were married?

In what ways do you see that your spouse has changed?

How do you feel about these changes?

What else would you like to see changed in your spouse?

In what ways have you shared your desires for change?

In what ways do you believe the past is affecting your present (past experiences, relationships, relatives/in-laws)?

What could you do to resolve these problems from the past?

List accomplishments and disappointments you have experienced as a couple:

Accomplishments:

Disappointments:

Describe the positive character traits of your spouse.

Describe the negative character traits of your spouse.

List your character traits as you know them.

Positive:

Negative: ______________________________

In what ways do you regard your spouse as an

Asset: ______________________________

Liability: ______________________________

What are the things you value most in life? (List in order of importance.)

1. ______________________________
2. ______________________________
3. ______________________________
4. ______________________________
5. ______________________________
6. ______________________________

What values do you not share with your spouse?

Values that I have that my spouse does not share: ______________________________

Values that my spouse has that I do not share: ______________________________

What goals are you pursuing as a couple? ______________________________

Which of your goals are not shared by your spouse? ______________________________

In what ways does your budget portray your goals and values? ____________________

What have you done to keep your marriage alive? (List specific things that only the two of you do together, such as going out to dinner, to concerts, retreats, trips, etc.) ____________________

What do you see as the basic needs of your spouse at this time (physical, emotional, financial, survival, security, significance, love, self-fulfillment, etc.)? ____________________

What have you done to assist him in getting his needs met? ____________________

What are your needs right now? ____________________

In what ways do you hope to have your needs met? ____________________

Counselor's Comments:

What We See in Each Other

Husband

Describe briefly your relationship to date in the following ways:

Positive experiences: __________

Negative experiences: __________

What premarital expectations have been fulfilled? __________

What premarital expectations have not been fulfilled?

In what ways have you changed since you were married?

In what ways do you see that your spouse has changed?

How do you feel about these changes?

What else would you like to see changed in your spouse?

In what ways have you shared your desires for change?

In what ways do you believe the past is affecting your present (past experiences, relationships, relatives/in-laws)?

What could you do to resolve those problems from the past?

List accomplishments and disappointments you have experienced as a couple:

Accomplishments:

Disappointments:

Describe the positive character traits of your spouse.

Describe the negative character traits of your spouse.

List your character traits as you know them.

Positive:

Negative:

In what ways do you regard your spouse as an

Asset:

Liability:

What are the things you value most in life? (List in order of importance.)

1.
2.
3.
4.
5.
6.

What values do you not share with your spouse?

Values that I have that my spouse does not share:

Values that my spouse has that I do not share:

What goals are you pursuing as a couple?

Which of your goals are not shared by your spouse?

In what ways does your budget portray your goals and values? ____________________

What have you done to keep your marriage alive? (List specific things that only the two of you do together, such as going out to dinner, to concerts, retreats, trips, etc.) ____________________

What do you see as the basic needs of your spouse at this time (physical, emotional, financial, survival, security, significance, love, self-fulfillment, etc.)? ____________________

What have you done to assist her in getting her needs met? ____________________

What are your needs right now? ____________________

In what ways do you hope to have your needs met? ____________________

Counselor's Comments:

SECTION II

What We Share Together

"Can two walk together, except they be agreed?" (Amos 3:3, KJV).

The writer of the book of Amos tells of the frustration of walking together for any length of time in a state of disagreement and disharmony. It is imperative that we learn how to share our lives together so that we grow together emotionally and spiritually. Signs of growing apart may take the form of frequent—and destructive—emotional storms; ever-increasing desert-like droughts in our relationship; a pattern of masking our true feelings; and an insistent searching for things and activities to fill the vacuum left by refusing the Lord's plan for our lives.

This section is designed to assist you in looking at the ways in which you share your life, and it underlines the necessity for an awareness of the spiritual dimension in life.

What We Share Together

Wife

Communication

Describe the content of your conversations in terms of major subject areas. (List in descending order, from most frequently discussed topics to least frequent.)

1. __________
2. __________
3. __________
4. __________
5. __________
6. __________
7. __________

In what ways have you had disagreements? __________

In what ways have you resolved your differences? __________

In what ways do you inform your spouse of your love for him?

In *words:* __________

In *actions:* __________

In what ways does your spouse inform you of his love for you?

In *words:* __________

In *actions:* __________

Do you feel that your spouse really listens to you and *understands* you and your needs? __________ Explain. ______

In what ways do you express your anger when you disagree? (Blow up or withdraw? Yell or cry? Seek quick solution or engage in prolonged pouting?) __________

Relational Issues

What does it mean to "love" someone? __________

What do you do to show you love your spouse? __________

In what ways do you want to be dependent/independent of your spouse?

Dependent: ______

Independent: ______

How close do you want your spouse to get to you?

1. List specific things in which you want your spouse to participate with you: ______

2. List specific things you want to do alone: ______

Do you ever fear being abandoned/divorced by your spouse? ______

If yes, how does this fear reveal itself in your relationship? ______

What would you do with your life if, for some reason, your spouse should die? ______

In what ways do you show emotional strengths/weaknesses?

Strengths: ______

Weaknesses: ____

In what ways do you use your strengths and weaknesses as a "power tool" to manipulate your spouse to do your bidding? ____

In what ways do you see your spouse using his strengths and weaknesses as a "power tool" to control you? ________

In what ways do you feel that your relationship is haunted by your parents' and your spouse's parents' marriage relationships?

Your parents: ____

Spouse's parents: ____

Spiritual Development

Do you believe in God? ________ If yes, what do you mean by "believe" and how has this belief concretely changed your life? ____

When do you believe you committed your life to the Lord? ____

Please explain what led up to this experience and its initial effects on your life. ______

Characterize the times when you felt closest to/farthest from God.

Closest: ______

Farthest: ______

How would you characterize your present Christian commitment (on a scale of 1 to 10, 1 being total indifference and 10 being fully committed)? ______ Explain. ______

In what ways have you grown/not grown spiritually?

Grown: ______

Not grown: ______

In what ways has your walk with God (or your lack of commitment) affected your relationship with your spouse?

In what ways do you see yourself as living consistently/inconsistently within the spirit of biblical principles?

Consistently: ______________________________

Inconsistently: ______________________________

In what ways do you perceive your spouse as being consistent/inconsistent in Christian living?

Consistent: ______________________________

Inconsistent: ______________________________

Portray a picture of God as you have experienced Him.

Attributes (God's qualities/personality—i.e., love, anger, etc.): ______________________________

Capabilities (God's power in the present—i.e., answered prayer, healing, revelation, etc.): ______________________________

Briefly portray the picture of God that you believe your spouse has, based on his experience of Him.

Attributes (His character—good/bad, loving/hateful, etc.): ______________________________

Capabilities (His power—strong/weak, active/inactive,etc.): ____________________

____

____

____

Counselor's Comments:

What We Share Together

Husband

Communication

Describe the content of your conversations in terms of major subject areas. (List in descending order, from most frequently discussed topics to least frequent.)

1. ______
2. ______
3. ______
4. ______
5. ______
6. ______
7. ______

In what ways have you had disagreements? ______

In what ways have you resolved your differences? ______

In what ways do you inform your spouse of your love for her?

In *words:* ______

In *actions:* ______

In what ways does your spouse inform you of her love for you?

In *words:* ______________________________

In *actions:* ______________________________

Do you feel that your spouse really listens to you and *understands* you and your needs? __________ Explain. ______

In what ways do you express your anger when you disagree? (Blow up or withdraw? Yell or cry? Seek quick solution or engage in prolonged pouting?) ______________________________

Relational Issues

What does it mean to "love" someone? ______________________________

What do you do to show you love your spouse? ______________________________

In what ways do you want to be dependent/independent of your spouse?

Dependent: ______________________________

Independent: ______________________________

How close do you want your spouse to get to you?

1. List specific things in which you want your spouse to participate with you: ______________________________

2. List specific things you want to do alone: ______________________________

Do you ever fear being abandoned/divorced by your spouse? ______

If yes, how does this fear reveal itself in your relationship? ______________________________

What would you do with your life if, for some reason, your spouse should die? ______________________________

In what ways do you show emotional strengths/weaknesses?

Strengths: ______________________________

Weaknesses: ______

In what ways do you use your strengths and weaknesses as a "power tool" to manipulate your spouse to do your bidding? ______

In what ways do you see your spouse using her strengths and weaknesses as a "power tool" to control you? ______

In what ways do you feel that your relationship is haunted by your parents' and your spouse's parents' marriage relationships?

Your parents: ______

Spouse's parents: ______

Spiritual Development

Do you believe in God? ______ If yes, what do you mean by "believe" and how has this belief concretely changed your life? ______

When do you believe you committed your life to the Lord? ______

Please explain what led up to this experience and its initial effects on your life.

Characterize the times when you felt closest to/farthest from God.

Closest:

Farthest:

How would you characterize your present Christian commitment (on a scale of 1 to 10, 1 being total indifference and 10 being fully committed)? ______ Explain.

In what ways have you grown/not grown spiritually?

Grown:

Not grown:

In what ways has your walk with God (or your lack of commitment) affected your relationship with your spouse?

In what ways do you see yourself as living consistently/inconsistently within the spirit of biblical principles?

Consistently:

Inconsistently:

In what ways do you perceive your spouse as being consistent/inconsistent in Christian living?

Consistent:

Inconsistent:

Portray a picture of God as you have experienced Him.

Attributes (God's qualities/personality—i.e., love, anger, etc.):

Capabilities (God's power in the present—i.e., answered prayer, healing, revelation, etc.):

Briefly portray the picture of God that you believe your spouse has, based on her experience of Him.

Attributes (His character—good/bad, loving/hateful, etc.):

Capabilities (His power—strong/weak, active/inactive, etc.): ______________________________

____

____

____

Counselor's Comments:

SECTION III

What We Expect of Each Other

"And whatever you do, in word or deed, do everything in the name of the Lord Jesus, giving thanks to God the Father through him" (Col. 17, RSV).

Almost everywhere we turn, we place a price tag on what we desire. We ask ourselves, "How much is this thing worth to me?" Sadly we do the same thing in our relationships. We are constantly asking the question, "What's in it for me?"

The problem with approaching relationships with ledger book and calculator is that it paralyzes us in truly loving our spouse. We cannot give of ourselves without dwelling on the return we will receive on our investment. We want a guarantee that any sacrifice on our part will be repaid with interest.

The Apostle Paul calls upon us to do all things, regardless of return, as a thank offering for God's acceptance of us, while we were yet unresponsive to Him. Work through this section, being sensitive to the fact that we do often approach our spouse with a ledger book and calculator. It is my hope that you will be able to exchange ideas and needs, and, as a result, you will seek to outgive each other! May each one of your acts of love become a way of saying "thank you" to the Lord for His love for you.

What We Expect of Each Other

Wife

Role Expectations as Husband/Wife

What do you feel should be the husband's role in a marriage? *Be specific.*

What do you feel should be the wife's role in a marriage? *Be specific.*

In what ways do your roles presently differ from what you believe they should be?

Role of husband:

Role of wife:

In what ways do you believe your roles have changed since you were first married?

In what ways do your work roles (whether in the home or outside the home) affect your relationship?

What steps could you take regarding your work to make your relationship better?

Who makes the major decisions in your relationship and what are your feelings about that arrangement?

Role Expectations as Parents

List your children in the following manner: names, ages , specific character traits unique to each one.

1. Name ________ Age ________
   Unique personality traits:

2. Name ________ Age ________
   Unique personality traits:

3. Name ________ Age ________
   Unique personality traits:

4. Name ______________________ Age ____________

Unique personality traits: ______________________

5. Name ______________________ Age ____________

Unique personality traits: ______________________

In what ways have your children been a blessing to you? ______________________

What specific problems have you had in raising your children? ______________________

What have you done about these problems? ______________________

What are your hopes and dreams for your children? ______________________

What do you see as your role in the disciplining of your children? ____________________

In what ways do you discipline? ____________________

What do you see as your spouse's role in the disciplining of your children? ____________________

In what ways does he discipline? ____________________

What do you see as the present needs of your children and what can you do to help them? (List individually.)

1. Name ____________________
   Needs: ____________________
   Ways of meeting those needs: ____________________
2. Name ____________________
   Needs: ____________________
   Ways of meeting those needs: ____________________
3. Name ____________________
   Needs: ____________________
   Ways of meeting those needs: ____________________
4. Name ____________________
   Needs: ____________________

Ways of meeting those needs: ______

5. Name ______
Needs: ______

Ways of meeting those needs: ______

What fun things do you do with your children to bring joy into their lives? (List the things you have done that you think were especially pleasant and memorable for your children.) ______

Do you approve of your children's friends? ______ What have you done to assist them in selecting "good" friends? ______

What is your role in the spiritual development of your children, and specifically what do you do to enhance this development? ______

What is your spouse's role in the spiritual development of your children, and specifically what does he do to enhance this development? ______

Sex Life

In what ways would you characterize your sex life as satisfying/unsatisfying (frequency, variety, achievement of physical-emotional-spiritual union)? ______

What do you do to remain sexually attractive to your spouse (physical fitness, grooming, clothing, mannerisms)?

What makes your spouse sexually attractive to you?

In what ways do you communicate to your spouse your interest in sexual intimacy (in terms of timing, setting, mood, attire)?

What "turns you on" sexually?

What "turns you off" sexually?

In what ways would you like to make your sex life better?

Have you discussed this with your spouse? ______ If yes, what was his reaction?

Is there any question of infidelity in your relationship? ______
If yes, how has this been dealt with?

Is there any question of homosexual inclinations in either yourself or your spouse? ______ If yes, how has it been dealt with?

Is there anything that has happened to you that inhibits you from relating in a sexually open manner with your spouse (i.e., childhood incest, premarital/extramarital relations, rape, fear of unwanted pregnancy/abortion)? ______

What do you believe it means to be sexually attractive as a man? ______

What do you believe it means to be sexually attractive as a woman? ______

Financial Worksheet

From your Budget Sheet, list in order of importance the main priorities in your life.

1. ______
2. ______
3. ______
4. ______
5. ______

If you are in debt, what did you do to get there and what steps are you taking toward debt reduction? ______

If someone gave you a gift of $5,000, how would you spend it? ______
Why? ______

What are your feelings about giving to church and charities? ____________________

____

____

____

____

Who is responsible for financial planning and bill paying in your home? ____________________

____

What are your financial goals? ____________________

____

____

____

____

What amount is allocated for you to spend freely as you choose? ________ What amount is allocated for your spouse to spend as he chooses? ________ If none is allowed, what amount would be appropriate for you to be able to spend freely? ________ For your spouse? ________ Do you have a savings plan? ________ Do you have life insurance? ________ If yes, list the amount and the beneficiary. ____________________

____

Do you have a will? ________ Does your spouse have a will? ________

What are your financial plans for the immediate future? ____________________

____

____

____

____

What effect do these plans have on your relationship with your spouse and your children? ____________________

____

____

____

Counselor's Comments:

What We Expect of Each Other

Husband

Role Expectations as Husband/Wife

What do you feel should be the husband's role in a marriage? *Be specific.*

What do you feel should be the wife's role in a marriage? *Be specific.*

In what ways do your roles presently differ from what you believe they should be?

Role of husband:

Role of wife:

In what ways do you believe your roles have changed since you were first married?

In what ways do your work roles (whether in the home or outside the home) affect your relationship? ______

What steps could you take regarding your work to make your relationship better? ______

Who makes the major decisions in your relationship and what are your feelings about that arrangement? ______

Role Expectations as Parents

List your children in the following manner: names, ages, specific character traits unique to each one.

1. Name ______ Age ______
   Unique personality traits: ______

2. Name ______ Age ______
   Unique personality traits: ______

3. Name ______ Age ______
   Unique personality traits: ______

4. Name ______________________ Age ______________

Unique personality traits: ______________________

5. Name ______________________ Age ______________

Unique personality traits: ______________________

In what ways have your children been a blessing to you? ______________________

What specific problems have you had in raising your children? ______________________

What have you done about these problems? ______________________

What are your hopes and dreams for your children? ______________________

What do you see as your role in the disciplining of your children? ______________________________

In what ways do you discipline? ______________________________

What do you see as your spouse's role in the disciplining of your children? ______________________________

In what ways does she discipline? ______________________________

What do you see as the present needs of your children and what can you do to help them? (List individually.)

1. Name ______________________________
   Needs: ______________________________
   Ways of meeting those needs: ______________________________

2. Name ______________________________
   Needs: ______________________________
   Ways of meeting those needs: ______________________________

3. Name ______________________________
   Needs: ______________________________
   Ways of meeting those needs: ______________________________

4. Name ______________________________
   Needs: ______________________________

Ways of meeting those needs: ____________________

5. Name ____________________
Needs: ____________________

Ways of meeting those needs: ____________________

What fun things do you do with your children to bring joy into their lives? (List the things you have done that you think were especially pleasant and memorable for your children.) ____________________

Do you approve of your children's friends? ______ What have you done to assist them in selecting "good" friends?

What is your role in the spiritual development of your children, and specifically what do you do to enhance this development? ____________________

What is your spouse's role in the spiritual development of your children, and specifically what does she do to enhance this development? ____________________

Sex Life

In what ways would you characterize your sex life as satisfying/unsatisfying (frequency, variety, achievement of physical-emotional-spiritual union)? ____________________

What do you do to remain sexually attractive to your spouse (physical fitness, grooming, clothing, mannerisms)?

What makes your spouse sexually attractive to you?

In what ways do you communicate to your spouse your interest in sexual intimacy (in terms of timing, setting, mood, attire)?

What "turns you on" sexually?

What "turns you off" sexually?

In what ways would you like to make your sex life better?

Have you discussed this with your spouse? ______ If yes, what was her reaction?

Is there any question of infidelity in your relationship?

If yes, how has this been dealt with?

Is there any question of homosexual inclinations in either yourself or your spouse? ______ If yes, how has it been dealt with?

Is there anything that has happened to you that inhibits you from relating in a sexually open manner with your spouse (i.e., childhood incest, premarital/extramarital relations, rape)? ______

What do you believe it means to be sexually attractive as a man? ______

What do you believe it means to be sexually attractive as a woman? ______

Financial Worksheet

From your Budget Sheet, list in order of importance the main priorities in your life.

1. ______
2. ______
3. ______
4. ______
5. ______

If you are in debt, what did you do to get there and what steps are you taking toward debt reduction? ______

If someone gave you a gift of $5,000, how would you spend it? ______

Why? ______

What are your feelings about giving to church and charities? ______________________________
____
____
____
____

Who is responsible for financial planning and bill paying in your home? ______________________
____

What are your financial goals? ____
____
____
____
____

What amount is allocated for you to spend freely as you choose? __________What amount is allocated for your spouse to spend as she chooses?__________If none is allowed, what amount would be appropriate for you to be able to spend freely? __________ For your spouse? __________ Do you have a savings plan? _____Do you have life insurance? _____ If yes, list the amount and the beneficiary. ______________________
Do you have a will? _____ Does your spouse have a will? _____
What are your financial plans for the immediate future? ______________________________
____
____
____
____

What effect do these plans have on your relationship with your spouse and your children? __________
____
____
____

Counselor's Comments:

BUDGET

Husband and Wife

Gross Income $ ________

Fixed Expenses:

Income and payroll taxes	$ ________
Social Security	________
Union Dues	________
Tithe (10% of Gross)	________
Other ________	________
________	________
Total Fixed Expenses	$ ________
Working Income (Deduct Total Fixed from Gross Income)	$ ________

Budget %

$________ Savings $ ________
(10% of Working Income)

$________ Living Expenses $ ________
(70% of Working Income)

	Monthly	Per Pay Period
Mortgage or Rent	$ ________	$ ________
Heat	________	________
Electricity	________	________
Water/Sewage/Garbage	________	________
Telephone	________	________
Car Insurance	________	________
Gasoline	________	________
Car Repairs	________	________
Recreation/Entertainment	________	________
Newspapers/Periodicals	________	________
Health Insurance	________	________
Car Insurance	________	________
Life Insurance	________	________
Doctor, Dentist, Medications	________	________
Food/Household	________	________
Cleaning/Dry Cleaning	________	________
Clothes	________	________
Home Furnishings	________	________
Emergency	________	________
Christmas and Gifts	________	________
Vacation	________	________
Allowances	________	________
Other ________	________	________
________	________	________
________	________	________
TOTAL LIVING EXPENSE	$ ________	$ ________

$________ Debts and Buffer (20% of Working Income)

________	________
________	________
________	________
________	________
________	________
________	________
________	________
________	________
________	________

TOTAL DEBTS $ ________ $ ________

SECTION IV

What We See as Our Needs

"Why do you see the speck that is in your brother's eye, but do not notice the log that is in your own eye?" (Matt. 7:3, RSV).

Our measure of other people, particularly those we live with, is not often accurate. Our perception is colored by past disappointments and disagreements, personal needs, idealistic fantasies about marriage, and limited understanding of the dynamics involved in two people becoming one.

Hopefully we can at least share with our spouse from our perspective on things. In that exchange of mental snapshots, we will begin to get a picture of reality. Once we have arrived at this, we can begin working on our problems.

I challenge you to deal with your problems as possibilities: possibilities to exercise faith which leads to greater spiritual maturity and opportunities to see God at work, truly making your relationship better.

What We See as Our Needs

Wife

State what you see as a major obstruction to growth in your marriage.

State what you believe your spouse sees as a major obstruction to growth in your marriage.

What has been done about your problem(s) to date?

What has *not* been done about the problem(s) that you believe should have been done by now?

What steps would you take to deal with the problem(s) and thus improve your relationship?

1.
2.
3.
4.
5.
6.
7.
8.

What steps do you believe your spouse should take to deal with the problem(s) and thus improve your relationship?

1. ______
2. ______
3. ______
4. ______
5. ______
6. ______

What goals would you set in the following areas?

Communication:

1. ______
2. ______
3. ______
4. ______
5. ______

Relations With Your Children:

1. ______
2. ______
3. ______
4. ______
5. ______

Finances:

1. ______
2. ______
3. ______
4. ______
5. ______

Vocational Goals:

1. ______
2. ______
3. ______
4. ______
5. ______

Sexual Life:

1. ______
2. ______
3. ______
4. ______
5. ______

Spiritual Life:

1. __________
2. __________
3. __________
4. __________
5. __________

Recreational/Leisure Time:

1. __________
2. __________
3. __________
4. __________
5. __________

Social Life/Friends:

1. __________
2. __________
3. __________
4. __________
5. __________

Counselor's Comments:

What We See as Our Needs

Husband

State what you see as a major obstruction to growth in your marriage.

State what you believe your spouse sees as a major obstruction to growth in your marriage.

What has been done about your problem(s) to date?

What has *not* been done about the problem(s) that you believe should have been done by now?

What steps would you take to deal with the problem(s) and thus improve your relationship?

1.
2.
3.
4.
5.
6.
7.
8.

What steps do you believe your spouse should take to deal with the problem(s) and thus improve your relationship?

1. ______
2. ______
3. ______
4. ______
5. ______
6. ______

What goals would you set in the following areas?

Communication:

1. ______
2. ______
3. ______
4. ______
5. ______

Relations With Your Children:

1. ______
2. ______
3. ______
4. ______
5. ______

Finances:

1. ______
2. ______
3. ______
4. ______
5. ______

Vocational Goals:

1. ______
2. ______
3. ______
4. ______
5. ______

Sexual Life:

1. ______
2. ______
3. ______
4. ______
5. ______

Spiritual Life:

1. ____
2. ____
3. ____
4. ____
5. ____

Recreational/Leisure Time:

1. ____
2. ____
3. ____
4. ____
5. ____

Social Life/Friends:

1. ____
2. ____
3. ____
4. ____
5. ____

Counselor's Comments:

SECTION V

What We Promise Each Other

"This is my commandment, that you love one another as I have loved you!" (John 15:12, RSV).

As you come to this last section, I am sure you are aware of all the times you have failed to keep your word. We live in a world of broken promises, ranging from unkept appointments to broken business and personal relationships. You may ask, "What value is there in my making another promise that may only be broken in the future?"

I would like to remind you that in this process of covenant-making, you are following God's commandment to love one another, and, therefore, are involved in a very sacred task. The Lord of love has not only given himself as our example, but He has also promised in His Word the power to do His will!

Since love is more than a feeling, carefully define the ways in which you will love and the ways you wish to be loved in your relationship. Do not make empty promises; but in measured fashion, declare what you meant when you first said, "I do."

What We Promise Each Other

Wife

Present Contract

WHAT I HAVE SAID (expectations *shared* with spouse)

I expect to give:

I expect to receive:

WHAT I HAVE THOUGHT (expectations *kept* inward)

I expect to give:

I expect to receive: ____________________

____

____

____

____

____

____

Instructions for the use of this contract negotiation sheet: Please fill out your initial feelings about what you would like to give and hope to receive in your marriage. After the sheets have been filled out on the left side, exchange with your spouse for his agreement or disagreement (to be filled out on the right side of this page). Note that there is a place for discussion (your questions, clarifications, qualifications and comments) as you agree/disagree with your spouse's expectations.

Contract Negotiation

Spouse's Responses

Agree Disagree

I would like to give . . .

1. ____________________ (1) ____________

____

____

2. ____________________ (2) ____________

____

____

3. ____________________ (3) ____________

____

____

4. ____________________ (4) ____________

____

____

5. ____________________ (5) ____________

____

____

Spouse's Responses

Agree Disagree

I would like to receive . . .

1. ____________________ (1) ____________

____

____

2. ____________________ (2) ____________

____

____

3. (3)

4. (4)

5. (5)

Spouse's Discussion (remarks, qualifications, clarifications on the agree/disagree responses):

Final Contract

I promise to love you in the following ways:

1.

2.

3.

4.

5.

I would like to be loved by you in the following ways:

1. ____

2. ____

3. ____

4. ____

5. ____

What We Promise Each Other

Husband

Present Contract

WHAT I HAVE SAID (expectations *shared* with spouse)

I expect to give: ______

I expect to receive: ______

WHAT I HAVE THOUGHT (expectations *kept* inward)

I expect to give: ______

I expect to receive: ____

____

____

____

____

____

Instructions for the use of this contract negotiation sheet: Please fill out your initial feelings about what you would like to give and hope to receive in your marriage. After the sheets have been filled out on the left side, exchange with your spouse for her agreement or disagreement (to be filled out on the right side of this page). Note that there is a place for discussion (your questions, clarifications, qualifications and comments) as you agree/disagree with your spouse's expectations.

Contract Negotiation

Spouse's Responses

Agree Disagree

I would like to give . . .

1. ______________________________ (1) ____________

____

____

2. ______________________________ (2) ____________

____

____

3. ______________________________ (3) ____________

____

____

4. ______________________________ (4) ____________

____

____

5. ______________________________ (5) ____________

____

____

Spouse's Responses

Agree Disagree

I would like to receive . . .

1. ______________________________ (1) ____________

____

____

2. ______________________________ (2) ____________

____

____

3. ____________________ (3) ________

4. ____________________ (4) ________

5. ____________________ (5) ________

Spouse's Discussion (remarks, qualifications, clarifications on the agree/disagree responses): ________

Final Contract

I promise to love you in the following ways:

1. ____________________

2. ____________________

3. ____________________

4. ____________________

5. ____________________

I would like to be loved by you in the following ways:

1. ______________________________

____

____

2. ______________________________

____

____

3. ______________________________

____

____

4. ______________________________

____

____

5. ______________________________

____

____

APPENDIX I

Counselor's Historical Summary

What We See in Our Past

Wife

Personal History

Name ____________________ Birthdate ____________________

Address ____________________ Age __________

Phone: Home ____________________ Business ____________________

Previously married? __________ If yes, how many times? __________

Duration of previous marriage(s) ____________________

Occupation ____________________ Years at that job ____________________

Name and address of employer ____________________

____

Education: Last year completed ____________________

Degree/diploma ____________________

Major and minor (if college) ____________________

Name and address of school ____________________

____

Other training: Type ____________________

Number of years or program ____________________

Name and address of school ____________________

____

Military Service: Branch ____________________ Rank ____________________

Number of years __________ Type of discharge ____________________

Special training ____________________

Have you ever been arrested? Yes ________ No ________

If yes, explain. ____________________

____

Have you ever or are you presently using agents that may induce chemical dependency? Yes ________ No ________

If yes, what drug have you used or what drug are you presently using? ____________________

Describe all important present or past illnesses or handicaps: ____________________

____

____

____

Have you ever been under treatment for emotional problems? Yes ________ No ________ If yes, describe when, where, how long, and under whose care: ____________________

____

Describe yourself in 150 words or less (what you would like people to know about you). ____________________

____

____

____

____

____

____

____

____

____

____

____

____

____

Describe the *best* thing that ever happened to you: ____________________

____

____

____

____

____

Describe the *worst* thing that ever happened to you: ____________________

____

____

____

____

____

Describe the person who has had the greatest influence on your life: ____________________

____

____

____

____

Family History

Father: Name ______________________ Living or deceased? ________

Occupation ______________________ Age ________

Education (highest grade completed) ______

Marital Status: Married ________ Separated ________

Divorced ________ Widowed ________

Marital History: Has your father ever been separated? ________

Divorced? ________ Widowed? ________

Mother: Name ______________________ Living or deceased? ________

Occupation ______________________ Age ________

Education (highest grade completed) ________

Marital Status: Married ________ Separated ________

Divorced ________ Widowed ________

Marital History: Has your mother ever been separated? ________

Divorced? ________ Widowed? ________

Description of Your Parents:

Father's character traits:

Positive: ____

____

Negative: ____

____

Mother's character traits:

Positive: ____

____

Negative: ____

____

In what ways do you believe you are like your parents?

Like your father? ____

____

____

Like your mother? ____

____

____

Description of Your Parents' Relationship:

Describe what you observed in the following areas of your parents' relationship:

Friendship/Companionship:

General characteristics: ____

____

Frequency of being together: ____

____

Intensity of relationship (competitive, combative, cool, casual, affectionate, romantic, etc.): ______

Sexual relationship: (Did you observe hugging, kissing, fondling, using endearing words, compliments, etc.?)

______

Decision-Making/Leadership Roles:

Who led and in what ways? ______

Religious Training in the Home:

Who trained and how? ______

Management and Finances:

Who managed the money, what did they do with the money, and how successful were they in this task? ______

Describe your relationship with your brothers and sisters during your childhood years: ______

Describe any major marital crises in your parents' marriage:

The conflict(s): ______

The reason for the conflict(s): ______

The resolution of the conflict(s): ______

Describe your feelings during this time: ______

In what ways are your feelings different today? ______

Were there any chemical dependency problems (either drugs or alcohol) in your family (parents, brothers, sisters)? Yes ______ No ______

If yes, how has that problem affected you? ______

Dating History

How did you meet? ______________________________

____

____

What initially attracted you to each other? ______________________________

____

____

____

How long did you date before you were engaged? ________

Did you date others prior to meeting your husband? Yes ________ No ________

If yes, how many others had you dated? ________ For how long? ________

How long were you engaged before you were married? ________

What made you decide to get married? (List five reasons in order of importance to you.)

1. ______________________________
2. ______________________________
3. ______________________________
4. ______________________________
5. ______________________________

Why do you think your spouse married you? ______________________________

____

____

____

What did you expect of marriage? Finish the statement:

"I expected to get

1) ______________________________
2) ______________________________
3) ______________________________

"I expected to give

1) ______________________________
2) ______________________________
3) ______________________________

When were you married? ______________________________

Where were you married? ______________________________

Who married you? (Name and address) ______________________________

____

How much premarital counseling did you have? ______________________________

What was the content of those sessions? ______________________________

____

Did you "love" one another when you were married? Yes ________ No ________

If yes, what do you mean when you say you "love" someone? ______________________________

____

____

What We See in Our Past

Husband

Personal History

Name ______________________ Birthdate ______________________
Address ______________________ Age __________
Phone: Home ______________________ Business ______________________
Previously married? ______________________
If yes, how many times? ______________________
Duration of previous marriage(s) ______________________
Occupation__________ Years at that job ______________________
Name and address of employer ______________________
____
____

Education: Last year completed ______________________
Degree/diploma ______________________
Major and minor (if college) ______________________
Name and address of school ______________________
____

Other training: Type ______________________
Number of years or program ______________________
Name and address of school ______________________
____

Military Service: Branch __________ Rank ______________________
Number of years __________ Type of discharge __________
Special training ______________________
Have you ever been arrested? Yes __________ No __________
If yes, explain. ______________________
____

Have you ever or are you presently using agents that may induce chemical dependency? Yes ______ No ______
If yes, what drug have you used or what drug are you presently using? ______________________
Describe all important present or past illnesses or handicaps: ______________________
____
____
____

Have you ever been under treatment for emotional problems? Yes ________ No ________ If yes, describe when, where, how long, and under whose care: ________

Describe yourself in 150 words or less (what you would like people to know about you). ________

Describe the *best* thing that ever happened to you: ________

Describe the *worst* thing that ever happened to you: ________

Describe the person who has had the greatest influence on your life: ________

Family History

Father: Name ______ Living or deceased? ______
Occupation ______ Age ______
Education (highest grade completed) ______
Marital Status: Married ______ Separated ______
Divorced ______ Widowed ______
Marital History: Has your father ever been separated? ______
Divorced? ______ Widowed? ______

Mother: Name ______ Living or deceased? ______
Occupation ______ Age ______
Education (highest grade completed) ______
Marital Status: Married ______ Separated ______
Divorced ______ Widowed ______
Marital History: Has your mother ever been separated? ______
Divorced? ______ Widowed? ______

Description of Your Parents:

Father's character traits:

Positive: ______

Negative: ______

Mother's character traits:

Positive: ______

Negative: ______

In what ways do you believe you are like your parents?

Like your father? ______

Like your mother? ______

Description of Your Parents' Relationship:

Describe what you observed in the following areas of your parents' relationship:

Friendship/Companionship:

General characteristics: ______

Frequency of being together: ______

Intensity of relationship (competitive, combative, cool, casual, affectionate, romantic, etc.): ____________

____

Sexual relationship: (Did you observe hugging, kissing, fondling, using endearing words, compliments, etc.?)

____

Decision-Making/Leadership Roles:

Who led and in what ways? ____________

____

____

Religious Training in the Home:

Who trained and how? ____________

____

____

Management and Finances:

Who managed the money, what did they do with the money, and how successful were they in this task? ______

____

____

____

Describe your relationship with your brothers and sisters during your childhood years: ____________

____

____

____

Describe any major marital crises in your parents' marriage:

The conflict(s): ____________

____

The reason for the conflict(s): ____________

____

____

The resolution of the conflict(s): ____________

____

____

Describe your feelings during this time: ____________

____

____

In what ways are your feelings different today? ____________

____

____

Were there any chemical dependency problems (either drugs or alcohol) in your family (parents, brothers, sisters)?

Yes ________ No ________

If yes, how has that problem affected you? ____________

____

____

____

Dating History

How did you meet? ______________________________

____

____

What initially attracted you to each other? ______________________________

____

____

____

____

How long did you date before you were engaged? ______________________________

Did you date others prior to meeting your wife? Yes ______ No ______

If yes, how many others had you dated? ________ For how long? ________

How long were you engaged before you were married? ____________

What made you decide to get married? (List five reasons in order of importance to you.)

1. ______________________________
2. ______________________________
3. ______________________________
4. ______________________________
5. ______________________________

Why do you think your spouse married you? ______________________________

____

____

____

What did you expect of marriage? Finish the statement:

"I expected to get

1) ______________________________

2) ______________________________

3) ______________________________

"I expected to give

1) ______________________________

2) ______________________________

3) ______________________________

When were you married? ______________________________

Where were you married? ______________________________

Who married you? (Name and address) ______________________________

____

How much premarital counseling did you have? ______________________________

What was the content of those sessions? ______________________________

____

Did you "love" one another when you were married? Yes ______ No ______

If yes, what do you mean when you say you "love" someone? ____

____

____

APPENDIX II

Group Leaders Discussion Guide

SECTION I — "What We See in Each Other"

What did you discover about each other in the following categories:

1. Positive and negative experiences
2. Expectations of marriage (before and after)
3. Feelings about change or lack of change in spouse
4. Ways the past has affected your hopes for the future
5. Character traits of self and spouse (positive/negative)
6. Values and goals of self and spouse (shared/not shared)
7. Needs of self and spouse (awareness of need and response to that need)

Group Leader's Notes and Comments: ______________________________

SECTION II — "What We Share Together"

1. What did you discover about the major content of your conversations?
2. In what major areas of life do you have disagreements with your spouse and how are these expressed? In what ways do you seek to solve these differences?

3. What did you learn by having to list the ways you love your spouse and he/she loves you in word and action?
4. What did you learn about each other's wishes to be dependent/independent of each other?
5. What did you learn about each other's strengths and weaknesses? In what ways does this affect your relationship?
6. What did you learn about each other's spiritual life in this exercise? In what ways do you believe you could help your spouse grow spiritually?
7. What did you learn about each other's view of God? In what ways do you believe each other's view of God impacts upon your life-style and relationship?

Group Leader's Notes and Comments: ______________________________

SECTION III – "What We Expect of Each Other"

1. What did you learn together in sharing your understanding of the roles of a husband and wife within a relationship?
2. What issues are you facing with your children which impacts on your lives? How are you dealing with these issues?
3. What do you see as the role of a husband/wife in raising children?
4. What makes your spouse attractive to you and what have you done to continue to encourage his/her interest in you? What "turns you off" concerning your spouse and what do you believe you can do to make your relationship better?
5. What do you believe it means to be sexually attractive as a man? As a woman?
6. What did you learn about each other's financial goals and priorities while working on the Financial Worksheet?

Group Leader's Notes and Comments: ______________________________

SECTION IV – "What We See as Our Needs"

1. In what ways do you believe you and your spouse need to grow (spiritually, emotionally, socially) and what steps do you think you must take to make it happen?
2. What goals for personal growth do you need to establish in the following areas: (Leader—go around the room by category and have each person list one thing from each category and share how he/she hopes to attain that goal.)
   a. Communication
   b. Relations with children
   c. Finances
   d. Vocational goals
   e. Relations with spouse
   f. Spiritual life
   g. Recreational/leisure time
   h. Social life/friendships

Group Leader's Notes and Comments:

SECTION V – "What We Promise Each Other"

1. What did you learn about your spouse and yourself in working through the contract exercise?

2. Discuss your expectations of your spouse and yourself in the give and take of marriage. (How does a couple negotiate differences—passive/aggressive roles?)
3. What does it mean to love and be loved by your spouse, now that you have been very specific in the contract section?
4. In what ways did this course help you?

Group Leader's Notes and Comments: ________________________________

APPENDIX I – "What We See in Our Past"

1. Who are you (birthplace, childhood, education, employment)? What are you (inward qualities—humor, honesty, diligence)? Where are you going (major goal in life)? How do you want to be remembered ("Here lies __________, who was ____________________.")?
2. In what ways has the past affected you both positively and negatively?
3. Describe your parents, their relationship, and how your marriage is like/not like theirs.
4. Describe how you first met and what attracted you to your spouse.
5. Why did you get married? (If answer is "we loved each other," encourage amplification of what they mean by "love.")

Group Leader's Notes and Comments: ________________________________